My Dog Buddy

Sunil Ram

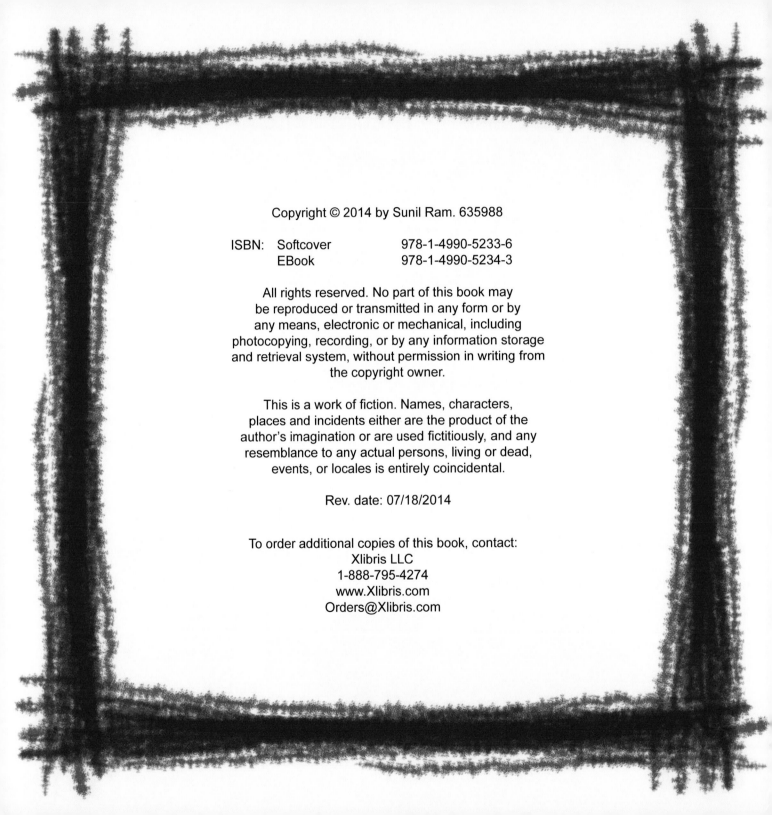

To order additional copies of this book, contact:
Xlibris LLC
1-888-795-4274
www.Xlibris.com
Orders@Xlibris.com

My Dog Buddy

Sunil Ram

Illustrations by Angel Dela Peña

I love my dog buddy.

Even when he's all muddy.

He always puts a smile on my face.

Even when he chews up my shoe lace.

I love the way he runs with his ball.

And I love that he always comes when I call.

I love that he never gets mad.

And licks my face whenever I'm sad.

One summer day, my mom brought him to the lake.

But she didn't realize that it would be a big mistake.

Because at the end of the day.

Buddy heard fireworks and ran away!

We searched everywhere up and down.

But buddy was nowhere to be found.

I kept searching left and right.

And called his name throughout the night.

It made me sad to be without my best friend.

And I was worried I would never see him again.

I couldn't believe he ran away without warning.

And that we still could not find him by the time it was morning.

So as I decided to go back home.

My mom got a call on her phone.

Buddy had been found safe and sound!

We all were so excited, jumping up and down!

We drove to the house where he was.

And I got out of the car to give him a big hug!

So for me, the day had a perfect end.

Because I was reunited with my best friend!

THE END

Printed in the United States
by Baker & Taylor Publisher Services